A postcard view of the Groudle Glen Hotel (opened 1893), the Manx Electric's first terminus. Winter saloon 9 of 1899, with trailer, sports a pair of original but short-lived bow collectors.

OLD TRAMS

Keith Turner

Shire Publications

CONTENTS

The horse era 3

Mechanical interlude 6

Electrification 12

Surviving tramways 19

The preservation movement 26

Further reading 31

Places to visit 32

ACKNOWLEDGEMENTS

Special thanks are given to all those who have so generously supplied photographs of trams in their possession. Photographs are acknowledged as follows: Beamish, North of England Open Air Museum, page 29 (upper); Margaret Donnison, pages 26, 27 (upper), 29 (lower), 30; East Anglia Transport Museum, page 25 (left); Glasgow Museum of Transport, pages 4, 28 (lower). Those on pages 1, 3, 5-11, 13-15, 17-19, 20 (upper) and 21 (lower) are in the author's collection. The remainder, including the cover, are by the author.

Cover: *Southampton 45 of 1903, the tram that started the modern preservation movement when it was saved from the scrapheap in 1948 by a group of enthusiasts. It is seen here at the National Tramway Museum at Crich on a hot August afternoon exactly half a century later.*

British Library Cataloguing in Publication Data: Turner, Keith, 1949-. Old trams. – 2nd ed. – (Shire album; 148). 1. Street railroads – Great Britain – History. I. Title. 388.4'6'0941. ISBN 0 7478 0409 5.

Published in 1999 by Shire Publications Ltd, Cromwell House, Church Street, Princes Risborough, Buckinghamshire HP27 9AA, UK. (Website www.shirebooks.co.uk)
Copyright © 1985 and 1999 by Keith Turner. First published 1985; reprinted 1989. Second edition 1999. Shire Album 148. ISBN 0 7478 0409 5.
Keith Turner is hereby identified as the author of this work in accordance with Section 77 of the Copyright, Designs and Patents Act 1988.

Printed in Great Britain by CIT Printing Services Ltd, Press Buildings, Merlins Bridge, Haverfordwest, Pembrokeshire SA61 1XF.

One of the Pwlhelli and Llanbedrog's primitive open cars in service during the 1920s. At the time of its closure in 1928 this was the last horse tramway still operating in the British Isles outside the Isle of Man.

THE HORSE ERA

The first tramway in Britain opened in the latter half of the nineteenth century, and most of its tramway systems had closed by the middle of the twentieth; the heyday of the tram was in the years immediately before and after the First World War, when, before the rise of the motor bus, it was the principal means of mass urban transport.

A tramway is basically a type of railway sharing a right of way with other road users; in Britain the first tramcar in the modern sense was operated by William Curtis over a goods line at the Mersey Docks in 1859. Other, purpose-built lines followed, promoted by the flamboyant American George Francis Train: Birkenhead in 1860, London the year after, and Darlington and the Potteries in 1862.

Other promoters began to show a cautious interest in this new form of transport. Each new line had to be authorised by a private (and costly) Act of Parliament, but in 1870, bowing to pressure, Parliament passed the Tramways Act, under the terms of which lines could be simply authorised by a Provisional Order (later confirmed by Parliament) of the Board of Trade. Ten years later some 250 miles (400 km) of tramways were in operation.

Horse haulage was the natural choice for the early tramways. On a paved surface free from the mud and ruts of the rest of the street a single horse could pull a double-deck tramcar – much to the disgust of the horse-bus owners, whose comparable vehicles required two or more animals to haul them (though several operators promptly changed sides!) – and was simply unhitched, walked round and reharnessed at the other end of its journey for the return trip. The wooden cars came in a variety of styles: double-deckers, open on top and glazed below, and single-deckers, open or glazed, were the two basic types. Popular at the seaside was the completely open 'toastrack', a platform with benches arranged across it.

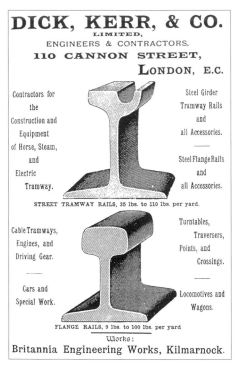

DICK, KERR, & CO.
LIMITED,
ENGINEERS & CONTRACTORS,
110 CANNON STREET,
LONDON, E.C.

Contractors for
the
Construction and
Equipment
of Horse, Steam,
and
Electric
Tramway.

Steel Girder
Tramway Rails
and
all Accessories.

Steel Flange Rails
and
all Accessories.

STREET TRAMWAY RAILS, 35 lbs. to 110 lbs. per yard.

Cable Tramways,
Engines, and
Driving Gear.

Cars and
Special Work.

Turntables,
Traversers,
Points, and
Crossings.

Locomotives and
Wagons.

FLANGE RAILS, 9 lbs. to 100 lbs. per yard.

Works:
Britannia Engineering Works, Kilmarnock.

Above left: The basic difference between railway and tramway rails can be seen in this 1890s advertisement from one of the major tramway construction companies of the time.

Above right: Representing the early years of electrification in Glasgow is car 779 of 1900. Like its horse-drawn predecessors it ran on four wheels and is similar in design to a horse-drawn car. It is now in the Glasgow Transport Museum.

A beautifully restored example of a typical double-deck two-horse tramcar. Dating from 1894, Glasgow 543 was originally built by the corporation for the North Metropolitan Tramways of London. Unlike most withdrawn cars, 543 was set aside as an exhibit when the system was electrified and is now also in the Glasgow Transport Museum.

An Edwardian postcard scene of Douglas Promenade on the Isle of Man, its majestic sweep typical of such major resorts of the period. Three of the horse tramway's many toastracks can be seen in service with, on the left, car 78 at the cable tramway terminus (note the conduit in the centre of the track).

The tramcars had four wheels with shallow flanges; these flanges ran in grooves along the tops of steel rails set flush into the road surface and so guided the car. (Early systems using other types of rail that protruded above the road surface were very unpopular with other road users and were soon abandoned.)

As with their railway counterparts, different gauges were used by different lines. (The gauge of a grooved-rail tramway is measured between the outside of the grooves, not between the insides of the rails as on a railway.) In practice a fairly logical pattern soon emerged in the British Isles: Irish tramways adopted either a 5 foot 3 inch (1600 mm) or a 3 foot (914 mm) gauge, these being the two railway gauges generally used in Ireland; the Isle of Man chose 3 feet (914 mm) for a similar reason, whilst in mainland Britain the three most popular choices were 4 feet 8^1/$_2$ inches (1435 mm, the standard railway gauge), 4 feet (1219 mm) and 3 feet 6 inches (1066 mm) for reasons of economy and scale. Some lines chose a different gauge, but these were a tiny minority.

Although possessing the virtues of simplicity and ease of operation, horse trams were slow, unsuitable for steep hills and a technological dead end. From the 1880s onwards they were rapidly displaced by other forms of traction and survived only on smaller and less intensively used urban systems, such as Oxford and Cambridge (both till 1914), or where their quaint appeal became a tourist attraction in itself, such as at Morecambe until 1926, Pwllheli until 1928 or Douglas to the present time.

Steam locomotive 'Sir Theodore' and train on the Glyn Valley Tramway, which converted from horse haulage to steam power in the 1880s. Two of the line's closed coaches are preserved (and operated) on the Talyllyn Railway.

MECHANICAL INTERLUDE

The tramway as we know it originated in the United States, where it was aptly termed a 'street railway', and the use of steam trams began there as well. From the late 1830s small locomotives had been used to haul tramcars, but by the 1850s the innovation had been made of installing a steam motor unit inside a passenger car. Both ideas were introduced to Britain within a few years of each other; in 1867 Manning, Wardle & Company of Leeds began exporting tramway engines, and in 1872 Merryweather & Sons of London constructed a powered passenger car which, after trials, went into service on the rural Wantage Tramway, then in Berkshire (now in Oxfordshire), four years later.

The use of steam on urban tramways was not permitted under legislation then in force, but, despite this, development continued in order to produce a safe machine capable of satisfying Parliament and the public. The idea of the powered passenger car was meanwhile abandoned in favour of a small locomotive (or dummy car) pulling a commodious trailer.

Several firms began to produce such engines. At first they were principally for export, but in 1879 the Act for the Use of Mechanical Power on Tramways allowed them on to British streets. (Their use had, however, been specially permitted on the Vale of Clyde Tramways two years previously.) During the 1890s they became a familiar sight, and at the time of their greatest popularity there were well over five hundred in service on some fifty different lines. After the experimental prototypes had been evaluated, most of the production models were very similar in appearance: squat, box-like machines with wrap-round metal skirts and a roof, through which a stub chimney poked, over a body almost totally open above the waistline. Inside was a small (usually two-cylinder) four-wheeled engine. The bodywork and skirts were to meet Board of Trade regulations (for public safety and silence), as

One of the very first users of steam power was the roadside Wantage Tramway, opened in 1875. Passenger services ceased in 1925, but goods traffic continued on the line for another twenty-one years. Railway-type tank engine 5 (built in 1857, bought second-hand and now preserved at Didcot Railway Centre) is seen here with trailers 4 and 5.

were the condensing apparatus for the exhaust steam and the use of coke instead of coal (both to reduce visible pollution). Dual controls enabled them to be driven from either end; the fireman remained at one end by the firebox. A speed limit of 10 miles (16 km) per hour – in a few cases even less – was imposed.

The carriages hauled as trailers were, at first, adapted horse cars. The intention originally was to use the power of the engines to haul a number of these coupled together like a train, but this was generally prohibited by local authorities and was put into practice only on rural lines that were virtually light railways. So, instead, the biggest possible single cars were especially constructed – usually double-deck bogie vehicles seating fifty or more. Trailers of this sort on the Wolverton & Stony Stratford Tramway

An advertisement from the 1890s for Bell Punch – probably the most famous name in the tramway ticket field – showing what the well-dressed employee was expected to look like.

Early picture postcards commonly featured local tramways and when a line or service closed the occasion would often be marked with a special card. This one commemorates the end of steam trams in Birmingham in 1906. The engine is a Kitson.

Befitting its position as the second largest city in Britain, Birmingham possessed the largest of all the 3 foot 6 inch (1066 mm) gauge systems, with over eight hundred cars. Typical of the fleet was United Electric car 146 of 1906, one of the many which ousted the steam trams.

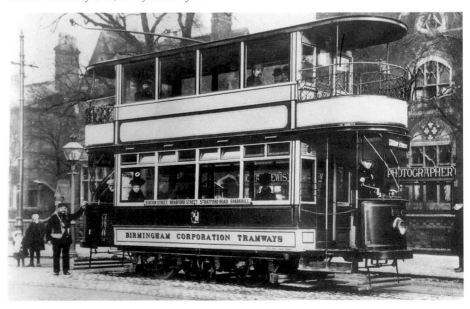

In Loving Remembrance of the
LEAMINGTON and WARWICK HORSE TRAMS,

Which

succumbed on

May 16th, 1905

to an

Electric Shock.

Aged 25 Years.

Let not ambition mock their useful toil,
Their homely joys, and destiny obscure.

Above: *In memoriam postcards were routinely issued to mark the end of horse or steam power on a town's tramway, usually – as in this case – replaced by electric traction.*

Worcester Electric Tramway Siege, 1903.

T. Bennett & Sons, Photographers,
Worcester and Malvern.

Left: *The physical conversion of a horse tramway to electric traction was a time of great upheaval. The changeover in Worcester, in 1903, was known as the Siege, and a series of postcards depicting the work in progress was issued locally.*

Souvenir postcards were also often produced to commemorate the grand opening of a town's electric tramway. This example is from Maidstone in Kent.

in Buckinghamshire – 44 feet (13.4 metres) long and nearly 6 feet (1.8 metres) wide (on a gauge of 3 feet 6 inches or 1066 mm) – seated one hundred passengers each and are believed to have been the largest tramway vehicles ever to run in Britain.

Just as steam had superseded horse traction on many lines, so it in turn gave way to the more efficient, cleaner, quieter and cheaper operation by electricity. The changeover was rapid. By 1910 the steam tram had vanished from the city streets; only on rural tramways that were virtually light railways did it survive long. (It was 1952 before the Wisbech & Upwell Tramway in the Fens replaced steam with diesel locomotives, and they too had to be modified to meet tramway regulations.) Unfortunately only a few items of stock – both locomotives and hauled vehicles – survive from this era today in preserved condition.

A widespread legacy of the steam tram is the bus stop. Horse trams, like cabs, could be hailed and boarded anywhere along the road. Steam trams, with their greater momentum, were not so easily stopped and started, and consequently the fixed tram stop, to the disgust of many, came into being. The idea was adopted by the electric lines and later by bus companies.

Shortly after the application of steam power to tramways came the cable system, which owed its practicality to a British invention of a means of gripping the cable. This was patented by William Curtis in 1838, though it was taken up first in the United States and developed there in the 1870s for use on the steep streets of San Francisco (where it survives as a tourist attraction) and other cities. It is a system ideal for such conditions. The cars themselves are not powered but fitted with grippers that engage a cable, in a conduit between the running rails, which is continuously driven from a winding house. When the conductor or driver engages the gripper the car is pulled along; when he disengages it the car runs free and, on application of the brake, stops.

The Lynton & Lynmouth Cliff Railway in North Devon began operation in 1890 as a conventional funicular railway except that the bodies of its two cars were actually small tramcars that could be wheeled off their platforms. This patented idea never caught on in Britain but was employed in other countries to enable tramcars (and their passengers) to be moved from one level of a tramway to another.

In Britain the system was confined primarily to lines on which the gradients precluded the use of steam traction. Short lines were opened up Highgate Hill in London (1884) and in Edinburgh (1888); the others that followed were in Birmingham (1888), Brixton (1892), Matlock (1893) and Douglas (1896). The Great Orme Tramway, described later, was the last cable tramway constructed in Britain but is worked on a different, simpler principle.

These tramways met with varying degrees of success. Where the need for a tramway was limited and could be adequately filled by just one line, a cable tramway could survive until forced to close by other external pressures. Thus the Matlock tramway lasted until 1927, the Douglas line until 1929. Where the line had to integrate with a wider network, however, one of three courses had to be taken. The first was to remain different and separate, resulting in inconvenience of interchange for passengers; no line took this course. The second was to give way to another system that could cope with both the other lines and the gradients of the cable line – namely electricity. The third option was to convert the adjacent lines to cable.

With the growing adoption of electric working from the 1890s onwards it was not long before the Brixton (1904), Highgate Hill (1909) and Birmingham (1911) lines were converted to it; in Edinburgh, however, the horse tramways were converted to cable working. The result was a complicated, unreliable system of junctions and crossovers that kept breaking down until it, too, was finally compelled – in 1922 – to convert to electric power.

ELECTRIFICATION

The history of the electric tramway is, for the early years, the history of the electric railway. Electric traction had been a theoretical possibility even in Faraday's time: in 1835 Thomas Davenport in the United States had built an electric 'locomotive' – a self-propelled motor on rails. The technological problems of the next decades were manifold, including how to generate enough current, how to supply the current to the motor and how to control the motor. They were not solved until the 1870s with the invention of the dynamo and the use of variable resistances as a control, thereby making an electrically powered rail vehicle a practical proposition.

In 1879 Dr Werner von Siemens opened the first viable electric railway. It was a short demonstration line at the Berlin Trade Exhibition with a third rail supplying the current, and it showed convincingly that electric traction was a practical idea. Two years later, also in Germany, the first electric street railway was laid, although, as it used one rail for current collection and one for return, it had to be fenced off from other road users. In 1883 Magnus Volk opened his narrow-gauge third-rail railway along the beach at Brighton, and in the same year the first electric tramway in the British Isles, the Giant's Causeway Tramway in Ulster, was opened. This used third-rail collection on the rural stretches and steam traction on the street sections and was eventually converted to the overhead wire system in 1899. The success of this line was followed in 1885 by the Bessbrook & Newry Tramway, also in Ulster, which used a third rail laid down the middle of the track as opposed to the outside of the running rails.

A live rail was not compatible with the tramway principle, however, since pedestrians and other road users had to be kept away from it. The ingenious answer adopted at Blackpool in 1885 was, in effect, to bury the conductor rail. A conduit in the centre of the track held two copper conductors, mounted on wooden boards, from which a metal plough suspended from the tramcar picked up the current. Unfortunately, despite draining into the town's sewerage system, the conduit often filled with sand, dirt and other foreign bodies, which not only blocked the progress of the ploughs but also frequently short-circuited the supply. This line, too, was converted to overhead working in 1889, but the possibility of the system had been shown and the third rail was thereafter used on railways, not tramways.

The conduit system was quickly superseded by the overhead, the only important exception being the London County Council's adoption of it: from 1903 on-

Trade advertisement for the (unsuccessful) Dolter surface-contact system of current supply, as used at Torquay and elsewhere.

The Kinver Light Railway in Staffordshire was, despite its title, an electric tramway and derived the bulk of its revenue from Black Country and Birmingham trippers to the village of its name. Car 6 of 1916 waits at the terminus beside evidence of the line's unusual goods service, the carrying of milk.

Apart from the clues given by the tram, this could be a scene from one of many industrial towns in the 1920s or 1930s. It is, in fact, Rotherham.

The elegance of the Edwardian seaside resort: two single-deck tramcars passing in Llandudno's main thoroughfare, unimpeded by the motor traffic that was later to bring about their demise here as well as virtually everywhere else in Britain.

wards over 120 miles (193 km) of route were electrified on this system to avoid the unsightliness of overhead wires. London apart, by the time of the First World War there were few tramways in Britain that did not use the overhead, with a direct current supply at 550 volts as the norm. It presented no danger to other road users, was easy to install and cheap to maintain. It was not nearly so prone to breakdown as the other electric systems but, if it did fail, it could be repaired without recourse to road works (a point very much in its favour with local authorities).

DECORATED CAR,
BIRMINGHAM CORPORATION TRAMWAYS.

Copyright.
ROYAL VISIT, July 7th, 1909.

Many tramways illuminated a car to mark special (usually royal) occasions. This Birmingham Corporation double-decker was so treated to mark the visit of King Edward VII and Queen Alexandra to open the University of Birmingham.

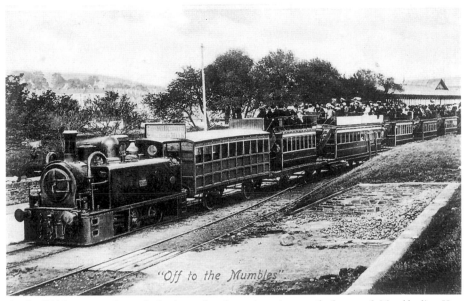

"Off to the Mumbles"

Another Welsh tramway that made the change from horses to engines was the Swansea & Mumbles line. Here locomotive 4 of 1899 heads a train laden with holidaymakers, a typical scene on this popular coastal line. One such train of twenty cars is recorded as carrying 1800 passengers – believed to be a world tramway record!

The principle of the overhead system had been demonstrated by von Siemens in 1881 (using a slotted-tube conductor), and the idea was taken up in the United States. Many design and technical problems had to be overcome, and the method of

In 1929 the Swansea & Mumbles line switched to electric traction, operating a fleet of 106-seater cars. These were some of the largest tramcars ever to run in Britain, and even then they often worked in coupled pairs, as here.

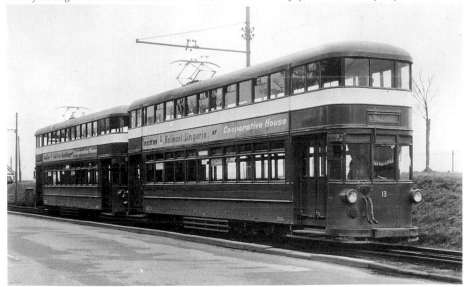

Left: *An assorted trio of works vehicles at the National Tramway Museum at Crich. Left is an English Electric locomotive of 1927 used at Blackpool to haul coal wagons; centre is a tower wagon for servicing the overhead, and right is Sheffield 330 of 1920, also built by English Electric, which began life as double-decker 251 at Bradford before conversion to a rail-grinding car at Sheffield in 1951.*

Right: *Motorists were not over-fond of tramcars – especially when they moved in to 'pinch' the unwary driver. This warning sign is now preserved at the East Anglia Transport Museum, Carlton Colville.*

current collection eventually perfected was to equip a tramcar with either a fixed frame (a pantograph or a bow collector) that rubbed against an overhead wire supported by roadside standards or, more commonly, with a trolley pole with a grooved wheel at the end held against the wire by a spring. Current return in both cases was via the running rails (as opposed to via a second overhead wire as used by trolleybuses).

The first overhead line in the British Isles (discounting the short stretches used at road crossings on the Bessbrook & Newry line) was opened at Leeds in 1891; next year came one at Bradford. Also in 1892 Guernsey switched from steam to the new system, and by the end of the decade it was in use almost everywhere.

In its design the electric tramcar owed much to its predecessors: single- or double-deck, open or closed, four- or eight-wheeled. Open cars were popular at seaside resorts, while fleets of cars seating sixty or so were the means of mass transport in the industrial cities. At each end of the car would be a driving position, where the driver stood (in the early days he would be lucky if he had the protection of a window above the dash); the motors were in the truck or bogies upon which the body was mounted, whilst the roof supported one or more current collectors.

Another method of electric working was the stud-contact system. Like the conduit system, this had the attraction of having no obtrusive wires and their standards in the streets. A supply cable buried beneath the centre of the track was connected at intervals to metal studs set flush into the road surface; when a tramcar passed over a

After the passing of the 1896 Light Railways Act many tramway systems were constructed under its provisions, hence the official title on Cheltenham 23 of 1921, here posed outside the depot and displaying a number of local advertisements.

A far cry from the systems of Britain's major towns and cities was the 2 foot (610 mm) gauge horse tramway that ran for less than 2 miles (3.2 km) from Fairbourne to the Mawddach estuary in mid Wales. Opened in 1898, it closed at the beginning of the First World War – to be rebuilt as a miniature railway that still operates (in a much modified form) today.

An immaculate Leicester Corporation tramcar of a pattern little changed from the first electric double-deckers apart from the protective provision of an upper deck roof (though the end balconies are still open) and windscreens for the driver.

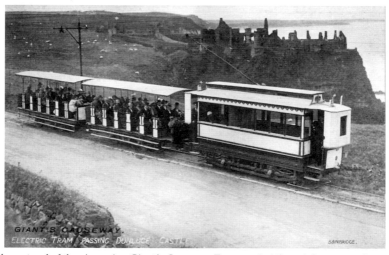

An early postcard of the pioneering Giant's Causeway Tramway in Ulster (after conversion to electric overhead working) with powered car 9 and two trailers passing Dunluce Castle on the line's spectacular coastal section.

stud, an electro-magnet on the car activated a small moving part in it, which completed a circuit to make the head of the stud live and so pass current, through a collecting skate, to the car. As the skate was long enough to connect with at least two studs at any one time, the current flow was – in theory – continuous. Return was through the running rails in the normal fashion.

Several undertakings adopted this system in the early years of the twentieth century. A number of different stud designs were tried, but all had the serious defect of sometimes staying live after a tram had passed, and the system was rejected in favour of the overhead within a few years. Lincoln (abandoned 1919) and Wolverhampton (1921) were the last two stud-contact operators.

SURVIVING TRAMWAYS

Tramways were ousted from British streets by the internal combustion engine. After the First World War the spread of the motor-car and motor-bus made the roads more crowded whilst public transport became more flexible. New bus routes could be opened quickly and cheaply and, for the local authorities of the day faced with the expense of replacing life-expired tracks and tramcars, switching to bus operation seemed an obvious solution. From the 1930s to the 1950s isolated lines and great networks alike were closed down one by one: for example, Rochdale in 1932, Derby in 1934, Birkenhead in 1937, Manchester in 1949, London in 1952 and Birmingham in 1953. Glasgow's survived until 1962. In the light of today's traffic problems in Britain and tramway experience in other countries, such a hasty closure programme was both illogical and disastrous.

There were few survivors.

BLACKPOOL

The world's oldest surviving electric tramway, and the first street tramway in Britain to be worked by electricity, was opened at Blackpool on 29th September 1885. Promoted by the Blackpool Electric Tramway Company, the 4 foot 8¹/2 inch (1435 mm) gauge line ran for a mile (1.6 km) along the promenade and used the conduit system of current collection. Acquired by the corporation in 1892, it was converted to the overhead system seven years later, and new town lines were added. In 1919 the corporation took over the neighbouring Blackpool to Fleetwood line (opened 1898) and began through running the following year.

Today the town lines have gone, but 11¹/2 miles (18.5 km) of tramway remain,

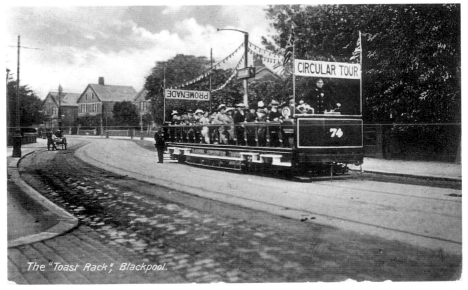

The "Toast Rack", Blackpool.

Blackpool 74 on a circular tour round the town, an excursion very popular with holidaymakers; weather permitting, so were tramcars of this open 'toastrack' pattern – so-called on account of their rows of cross benches for the passengers. (This part of the Blackpool system is now closed.) One of the later toastracks, 166 of 1927, is preserved at Crich.

The tram that went to sea: the Brighton & Rottingdean Seashore Electric Tramroad was arguably the oddest tramway ever built. Its one car – named 'Pioneer' – ran on parallel tracks along the edge of the sea. Operating from 1896 to 1901, it was not a success!

giving joyrides to thousands every summer and providing a swift and regular communication with Fleetwood all the year round. The passenger fleet consists of over seventy bogie vehicles, both single- and double-deck, ranging from the English Electric 'Boats' of 1934 (so called after their open boat-like appearance) to the Blackpool-built one-man cars of recent decades. Five cars, rebuilt in 1959-65, carry illuminated bodywork of various designs (including a Wild West train and a space rocket).

One of the benefits gained from Blackpool's long run of service, together with its welcome policy of reluctance to scrap withdrawn cars, is that many of its trams have survived for preservation elsewhere. In return, Blackpool operates a number of preserved cars on loan from elsewhere, enabling visitors to see them working once more in an urban setting.

GREAT ORME TRAMWAY

The last remaining tramway in Wales winds its way through the back streets of Llandudno, climbing all the while, and out on to the open slopes of the Great Orme, the massive limestone headland looming over the town. At 650 feet (198 metres) above sea level, Summit station is only 29 feet (9 metres) below the Orme's highest point; in

Blackpool has been a fruitful source of tramcars for preservation; seen here at the East Anglia Transport Museum, number 11 of 1939 was acquired when withdrawn in 1965.

Blackpool 159 of 1927, also at the East Anglia Transport Museum. A member of the Blackpool 'Standard' class, it ran from 1959 to 1966 as one of the famous illuminated cars.

little under a mile the 3 foot 6 inch (1066 mm) gauge line has climbed 561 feet (171 metres), an average gradient of 1 in 9 (and including a stretch of 1 in 3.6 on the lower section).

The tramway is cable-worked on the funicular railway principle, with the cars permanently attached to the cable; the winding house is sited at Halfway station and physically divides the line into two sections. The lower half of the line, commencing at Victoria station on the corner of Old Road and Church Walks, is paved, with the cable running in a conduit, whilst on the upper half from Halfway to Summit the track and cable are exposed. The two sections opened in 1902 and 1903 respectively and, since 1903, services have operated in the summer months only.

Cars nos. 4 and 5 work the lower section and nos. 6 and 7 the upper. All were constructed by the Motherwell firm of Hurst, Nelson & Company for the opening and are identical bogie carriages seating forty-eight. The window spaces are unglazed. The same firm also supplied cars nos. 1, 2 and 3, small four-wheeled cars for carrying coke up to the winding house and supplies to the hotel at the summit. (At one time a loop line and siding connected the two sections of the tramway at Halfway.) They were also used as hearses to transport coffins up to St Tudno's churchyard on the Orme. All three vehicles, which when in service were pushed up

The 1950s saw the last wave of tramway closures in England, with scenes like this 'Last Tram' day in Liverpool repeated up and down the country. Car 293 was one of the 'Baby Grand' class of streamliners constructed between 1937 and 1942 by the corporation.

21

Victoria station on the Great Orme Tramway in 1974 with car 5 (Hurst, Nelson of 1902) awaiting passengers for the ride to the summit. The station dates from 1904 and is immediately below the site of the 1902 terminus. Note the 'Great Orme Railway' sign – the tramway's title from 1935 to 1976.

the line by one of the other cars, have since been scrapped.

The trolley poles on the tramcars' roofs were formerly used to make telegraphic communication with the winding house via an overhead wire, but this is now done by means of radios. Since 1991 the cars have carried names – an unusual but not historically unique occurrence on British tramways. They are *St Tudno* (no. 4), *St Silio* (no. 5), *St Seriol* (no. 6) and *St Trillo* (no. 7), all names of former North Wales coastal steamers.

Cable car 4 (Hurst, Nelson of 1902) making the descent of the lower section of the Great Orme Tramway beside Tygwyn Road; the gradient of the line is not exaggerated by the camera. The hand brake by the driver's left hand is not used during normal running; instead the cable is halted and released at the winding house.

Laxey station on the Isle of Man with, from left to right, Snaefell Mountain Railway 3 (Milnes of 1895), Manx Electric motor saloon 7 (Milnes of 1894) and unpowered trailer 45 (Milnes of 1899). The view is looking north; the Snaefell line dispenses with the Fell centre rail in the station.

DOUGLAS

Douglas, the capital of the Isle of Man, is the home of Britain's last horse tramway. The line has survived for several reasons: firstly, Douglas is predominantly a holiday resort, and the horse trams quickly became one of its attractions; secondly, people use the line to enjoy the air along the sea-front or to reach their hotel, and its leisurely pace is well suited to its riders; and thirdly, being confined to the sea-front, it interferes little with the traffic of the town. So it has remained relatively unchanged since it opened in 1876, while the horse tramways of the mainland have long since vanished.

Laid on the 3 foot (914 mm) gauge, the original single line was later extended and doubled until by 1890 it had reached its present length of 2 miles (3.2 km); in 1901 it was purchased by the corporation. Winter services ceased in 1955 (displaced by motor-buses), and the tramway now operates during the summer months only but even so carries half a million passengers a year. At peak times there is a service of at least one car every two minutes; such a demand is met by having at least twenty cars ready for use at any one time and twice that number of horses. All the cars are single-deckers from a variety of builders, with the exception of no. 14, an 1883 double-decker that has been restored for use on special occasions. The car depot at Derby Castle is normally open to visitors and houses a display of Douglas cable tramway relics plus that line's beautifully restored car 72/73 (so numbered because it was reconstructed from those two derelict cars), which is now battery-powered so that it can be worked along the horse tramway on special occasions.

MANX ELECTRIC

Unlike the Douglas horse trams the Manx Electric Railway, a 3 foot (914 mm) gauge overhead electric tramway, serves a real local transport need in addition to its function as a tourist attraction. As a result it has come increasingly into competition with motor transport on the island, and since the Second World War there has often been the threat of closure. Happily the present policy of vigorous promotion of the line has reduced this threat.

The first section of the tramway was opened from Derby Castle, at the northern end of Douglas Bay (and now the terminus of the horse tramway), to Groudle Glen, 2 miles (3.2 km) up the coast, in 1893. In the following year the track was doubled and by 1899 the final destination, Ramsey, nearly 18 miles (29 km) from Douglas, had been reached. In 1957 the line was taken over by the Manx government and is

A rare sight on a British tramway: a goods vehicle. This is Manx Electric mail van 16 at Ramsey. The van was built in 1908 by the MER at Derby Castle, together with similar vehicle 15. Mail services ceased in 1975.

now part of Isle of Man Railways.

A trip on the MER is one of the delights of a visit to the island. Laxey station, 7 miles (11 km) from Douglas, is surely the pleasentest of all tramway stations whilst the sea views between there and Ramsey are spectacular.

Trams currently run from spring to autumn, with the service frequency determined by the time of year and traffic demands. Each tram usually consists of a powered car and a trailer – the line has twenty-four of each – running as a unit. The oldest cars date from the opening of the line, the most modern from 1930, and – rarely for a tramway – a number of original goods vehicles also exist. A small museum at Ramsey station houses stock and relics from the tramway.

SNAEFELL

Although technically a railway, the Snaefell line in the Isle of Man – officially entitled the Snaefell Mountain Railway – is included here because it is operated with tramcars very similar to some of those of the Manx Electric Railway, a line with which it has always had close connections. It was opened in 1895 by the Snaefell Mountain Railway Association and is unique in the British Isles in that it uses the Fell centre-rail system, whereby a raised central rail is engaged by brake equipment in the car bogies in order to prevent a runaway descent. Normal adhesion is sufficient to make the 1 in 12 ascent. The gauge is 3 feet 6 inches (1066 mm), rather than the Manx standard of 3 feet (914 mm), in order to accommodate the centre-rail equipment, and the cars are electrically powered via an overhead supply.

The original six cars, built by G. F. Milnes & Company and numbered 1 to 6, are still in use. They were identical single-deck vehicles when delivered (each seating forty-eight passengers) and had clerestories added to the roofs in 1897. After catching fire in 1970, no. 5 was rebuilt without this feature, and between 1979 and 1982 all six were fitted with full rheostatic braking equipment.

Soon after its opening the line passed into the hands of the MER's owners and since then has been worked in conjunction with that line (though with a slightly shorter operating season and services subject to the weather). Commencing at Laxey station on the MER, the railway spirals round Snaefell for 4³/₄ miles (7.6 km) to reach a terminus 1992 feet (607 metres) above sea level just below the highest point on the island, 2036 feet (621 metres) above sea level, from where, on a clear day, England, Wales, Scotland and Ireland can all be seen.

SEATON

Although it is not strictly a surviving early tramway, the Seaton & District Tramway in Devon possesses an intriguing history. It had its origin in 1948 when Mr C.

Above left: *A typical Edwardian open-topper: Lowestoft 14 of 1904. Built by Milnes for the 3 foot 6 inch (1066 mm) gauge, it was sold when the system closed in 1931 and became a summerhouse. Now at the East Anglia Transport Museum, it has been remounted on a standard-gauge truck from Sheffield.*

Above right: *Glasgow 812 in service at Crich. Built in 1900 as an open-top car, it was modified and updated over the years and was not withdrawn until 1960, when it was saved for preservation. It now runs in yellow livery – Glasgow painted its trams according to the route they operated.*

W. Lane of New Barnet, an engineer and manufacturer of battery-electric road vehicles, constructed a one-third scale working model of a Llandudno & Colwyn Bay tramcar. A closed 15 inch (381 mm) gauge double-decker, it had two decks inside for the somewhat cramped passengers.

The first stretch of track was laid in the yard of Mr Lane's works; this was followed in 1949 by a temporary track and overhead that could be taken to fetes and similar events. A unique line such as this seemed to have a promising commercial future, and so a more permanent site was sought. After trials in 1951 at St Leonards, in 1952 a quarter-mile (400 metre) line was opened in Voryd Park, Rhyl, with three (later four) tramcars. In 1955 the tramway moved to Eastbourne, and new cars, more narrow-gauge than miniature, were constructed for a new gauge of 2 feet (610 mm), using wherever possible controllers and fittings from scrapped full-size trams.

Profitable operations continued until the late 1960s when local development curtailed the company's activities. A new site was then chosen: part of the abandoned railway branch line from Seaton Junction, near Axminster, to the south Devon coastal resort of Seaton. A new gauge of 2 feet 9 inches (838 mm) was adopted to permit the use of still larger tramcars. The 1 mile (1.6 km) Eastbourne line closed in 1969, and the first stretch of the Seaton line opened the next year; gradual extensions have now completed the 3 mile (4.8 km) line from Seaton to Colyton.

A summer-only service is operated using a total fleet of some ten passenger cars, both single- and double-deckers, of which one, no. 14, is a 1984 rebuild of a 1905 car that formerly ran as the standard-gauge Metropolitan Electric Tramway's no. 94, whilst no. 16 is a 1992 rebuild of Bournemouth 106 of 1921 vintage. The latest car to enter service (in 1998) is no. 19, a rebuild of the 1906 Exeter car of that number. (These two latter systems were both of 3 foot 6 inch, 1066 mm, gauge.) A fleet of assorted works vehicles reinforces the point that, although of very narrow gauge, the Seaton line is a genuine tramway with a long and continuing history of its own.

A busy moment on the museum line at Crich with Paisley 68 of 1919 waiting to be passed.

THE PRESERVATION MOVEMENT

The preservation of tramcars has been going on for many years, with withdrawn vehicles being saved from the scrapheap by a wide variety of operators, preservation groups and private individuals. Unlike the railway preservation movement, however, no actual line has been preserved – the closest example being the Heaton Park Tramway in Manchester, which has been laid on the site of a former corporation siding. Other such lines may perhaps be opened in the future, but they will almost certainly have to be reserved rights of way not open to other road traffic. In one sense, the older surviving tramways are now preserved tramways in their own right since they have become increasingly 'pleasure' rather than 'public transport' orientated, their aging tramcars objects of nostalgia.

Elsewhere, the recent trend has been not just to preserve tramcars in museums but to lay exhibition lines for them to run on. Other than the Heaton Park line, preserved trams can now be ridden at the Black Country Museum at Dudley (services commenced 1980); Beamish, the North of England Open Air Museum, County Durham (1973); the East Anglia Transport Museum near Lowestoft (1972); and, with by far the largest vehicle collection of all, the National Tramway Museum at Crich, Derbyshire (1963).

The idea of a National Tramway Museum dates back to 1955, when the Tramway Museum Society was formed to save what it could from Britain's rapidly vanishing tramways; in 1959 the Crich site, in a limestone quarry, was acquired with the long-term aim of running restored tramcars over a fully operational electric tramway.

The standard gauge of 4 feet $8^1/2$ inches (1435 mm) was chosen for the new line as it suited the greater number of trams collected, and in 1963 a horse tram service was inaugurated over the first section. By the following year the overhead was sufficiently complete to enable the first electric cars to run, since when the line has been extended to a mile (1.6 km) in length. At the museum end a variety of items has been assembled to recreate a typical Edwardian street scene. Only one or two of the more than fifty British and foreign tramway vehicles at the museum are in operation at normal times; the majority of the others can be inspected in the sheds, though on

Electric tramway locomotives were always rare on British tramways. This is the Manx Electric's unique no. 23 of 1900, seen here at Laxey in 1993, in rebuilt form after restoration (and named for the line's centenary celebrations).

summer Sunday afternoons, bank holidays and special event days a greater number are running.

Compared with the expense of restoring and running a main-line steam locomotive, preserving a tramcar is a low-cost, though still expensive and time-consuming undertaking, and the rescue and rebuilding of long-abandoned vehicles continues. This is possible because it was common practice for withdrawn trams to be stripped of their control and running gear (for either reuse or scrap) and the bodies sold to become garden sheds, cricket pavilions or whatever – only to be discovered decades later.

One last tramway, opened in 1995 in Birkenhead, needs to be mentioned. Known as the Wirral Tramway, and operated by Blackpool Transport Services on behalf of Wirral Metropolitan Borough Council, it runs for some 400 yards (365 metres) on a roadside reservation from the Woodside ferry terminal along Shore Road to Pacific Road, a location fittingly that of part of George Francis Train's pioneering 1860 line. The single track is laid with rails salvaged from the Liverpool tramway system, and the two cars, numbered 69 and 70 to continue the old Birkenhead tramways fleet list, were

Liverpool 869, built in 1936 as one of the 'Green Goddess' class intended for an extensive modernisation programme of the city's tramways. After the Second World War many were sold to Glasgow and for a while 869 ran there as number 1055. It is now preserved at Crich.

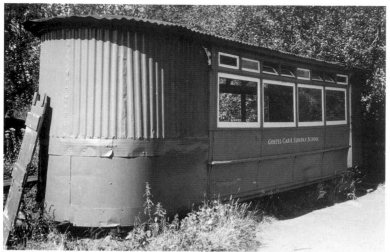

This car body from the extensive Black Country electric tramway network was used as a chapel and Sunday School after with-drawal from service. It is now preserved in that form at the Blists Hill Open Air Museum, Ironbridge, Shropshire.

purpose-built in Hong Kong (another port with a long tramway tradition). They are enclosed double-deckers deliberately designed to be slightly antiquated, rather than modern, in appearance. The intention was to extend the line as part of a docks regeneration scheme, but whether this will ever happen is doubtful. Even if it does not, similar 'heritage' lines may very well be constructed elsewhere as features of such urban developments to blur even further the distinctions between real and replica, old and new, preservation and pleasure. It would seem that the future of 'old trams', in the broadest of senses, is a bright one.

Last of the Glasgow-built 'Cunarders', no. 1392 dates from 1952 and represents the very last stage of tramcar design there. It is now on show in the Glasgow Museum of Transport.

Gateshead 10 of 1925 is now operational once more at Beamish, the North of England Open Air Museum. Withdrawn in 1951, it was purchased by British Railways and ran on the Grimsby & Immingham Light Railway as no. 26 until 1961, when that line also closed.

The very first tramcar to run in service at the National Tramway Museum, Crich, was Sheffield horse car 15 of 1874, seen here in one of the modern car sheds.

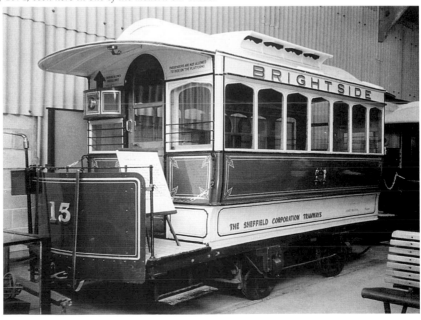

Above: Showing very little difference in its single-deck design despite being a quarter of a century older, Chesterfield horse car 8 of 1899, also beautifully restored and on show at Crich.

Left: London County Council 106 of 1903 in service at Crich. For many this is still the image conjured up by the word 'tram'.

FURTHER READING

Collins, Paul. *The Tram Book*. Ian Allan, 1995. A look at British tramway history with the emphasis on some of its more neglected aspects as well as a general overall picture.

Gill, Dennis. *Heritage Trams*. Trambooks, Stockport, 1991. An invaluable guide to working and preserved stock in the British Isles.

Johnson, Peter. *British Trams and Tramways in the 1980s*. Ian Allan, 1985. A guide to Britain's working and museum tramways.

Turner, Keith. *The Directory of British Tramways*. Patrick Stephens, 1996. Comprehensive encyclopedic coverage of all the passenger-carrying tramways, past and present, in the whole of the British Isles.

Waller, Michael H. and Peter. *British and Irish Tramway Systems since 1945*. Ian Allan, 1992. Concise but detailed accounts of all the tramways of the British Isles still operating after the end of the Second World War.

All aspects of the modern tramway scene worldwide are covered by the magazine *Tramways & Urban Transit* (formerly *Modern Tramway*), published jointly by the Light Rail Transit Association and Ian Allan Ltd and available through newsagents and specialist bookshops. The LRTA also publishes the quarterly journal *Tramway Review*, which concentrates on historical matters.

Histories of individual lines and regional systems are too numerous to list here. Some are published by their authors themselves whilst many others come from local authorities and local history publishers, from dedicated groups such as the Light Rail Transit Association and the Tramway and Light Railway Society, or from transport imprints with national coverage such as the Oakwood Press, Ian Allan and the Middleton Press. (Advertisements for these, together with reviews of new works from all sources, appear regularly in *Tramways & Urban Transit*.)

Britain's last horse tramway in action: Douglas all-weather car 50 under way. Built in 1935 by the Vulcan Motor & Engineering Company, it was originally fitted with side screens for use in bad weather.

PLACES TO VISIT

Tramcars surviving as public transport can be ridden on:

Blackpool & Fleetwood Tramway, Blackpool Transport Services, Rigby Road, Blackpool FY1 5DD. Telephone: 01253 473001.

Great Orme Tramway, Victoria Station, Church Walks, Llandudno. Telephone: 01492 574237.

Douglas Horse Tramway, Strathallan Crescent, Douglas, Isle of Man IM2 4NR. Telephone: 01624 675222.

Manx Electric Railway, address as above. Telephone: 01624 663366.

Snaefell Mountain Railway, address as above. Telephone: 01624 663366.

Seaton & District Tramway, Harbour Road, Seaton, Devon EX12 2NQ. Telephone: 01297 20375. Website: www.tram.co.uk

Working preserved tramcars can be experienced at:

Beamish, North of England Open Air Museum, Beamish, County Durham DH9 0RG. Telephone: 01207 231811. Website: www.merlins.demon.co.uk/beamish

Black Country Living Museum, Tipton Road, Dudley, West Midlands DY1 4SQ. Telephone: 0121 557 9643. Website: www.bclm.co.uk

East Anglia Transport Museum, Chapel Road, Carlton Colville, Lowestoft, Suffolk NR33 8BL. Telephone: 01502 518459 (info line). Occasional opening only.

Heaton Park Tramway, Manchester. Operates Sundays and bank holidays spring to autumn, plus summer Wednesdays.

National Tramway Museum, Crich, Matlock, Derbyshire DE4 5DP. Telephone: 01773 852565. Website: www.tramway.co.uk

Summerlee Heritage Park, Heritage Way, Coatbridge, Lanarkshire ML5 1QD. Telephone: 01236 431261.

'Heritage' tramcars can be ridden on:

Wirral Tramway, Woodside Ferry Terminal, Birkenhead. Telephone: 0151 647 6780. Operates weekends and school holidays only.

Many British museums contain static tramcars and other tramway exhibits, usually with local associations. Major collections of vehicles can be seen at:

Glasgow Museum of Transport, 1 Bunhouse Road, Glasgow G3 8DP. Telephone: 0141 287 2720.

Hull Transport Museum, High Street, Hull HU1 1NG. Telephone: 01482 613956. Website: www.hullcc.gov.uk/museums

London Transport Museum, 39 Wellington Street, Covent Garden, London WC2E 7BB. Telephone: 0171 379 6344 or 0171 565 7299 (info line). Website: www.ltmuseum.co.uk

Ulster Folk and Transport Museum, Cultra, Holywood, County Down BT18 0EU. Telephone: 01232 428428.

Other places with interesting tramway vehicles include:

Milton Keynes Museum, McConnell Drive, Wolverton, Milton Keynes MK12 5EJ. Telephone: 01908 316222. Website: www.artizan.demon.co.uk/mkm (A Wolverton & Stony Stratford double-deck steam tramcar, thought to have been the last working steam tram in Britain.)

Southern Electric Museum, The Old Power Station, Bargates, Christchurch, Dorset BH23 1QE. Telephone: 01202 480467. (The only remaining Bournemouth Corporation tram.)

Talyllyn Railway, Wharf Station, Tywyn, Gwynedd LL36 9EY. Telephone: 01654 710472. Website: www.talyllyn.co.uk (Operates two former Glyn Valley Tramway coaches as part of its stock.)